THINGS ART TEACHERS Really WANT TO Say But Can't

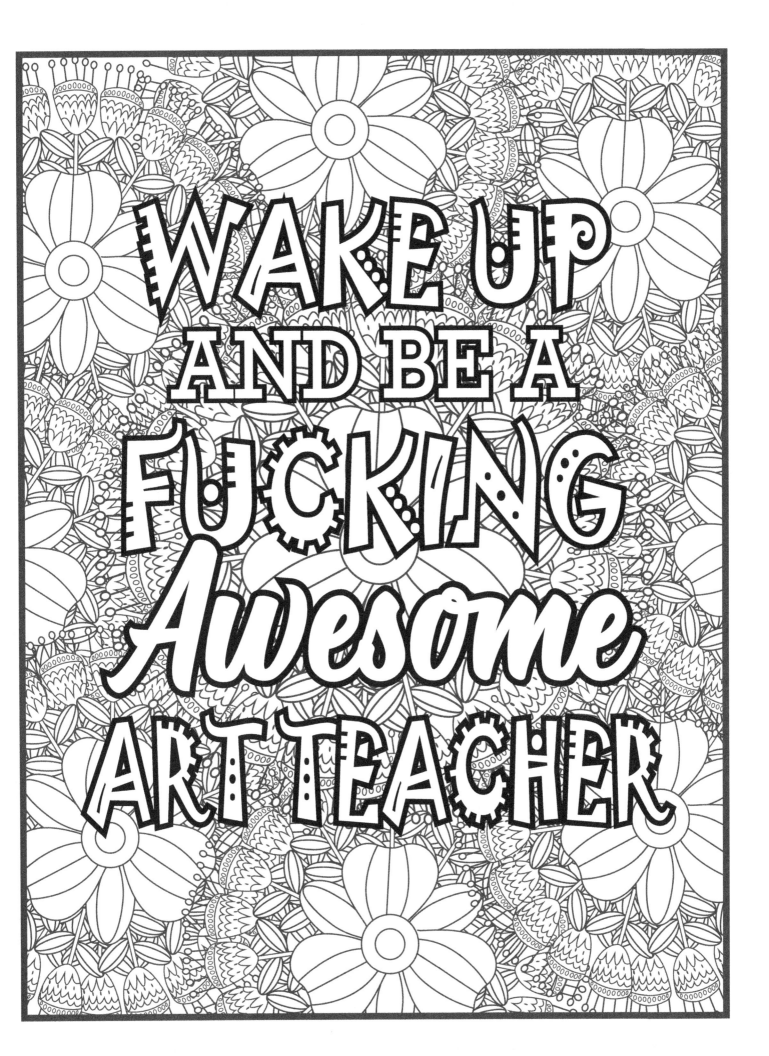

THANKS FOR CHOOSING Our COLORING BOOK.
WE TRULY HOPE THE RECIPIENT OF THIS
BOOK GETS A FEW LAUGHS FROM THE QUOTES INSIDE.
AS A SMALL BUSINESS SELLING ON AMAZON,
YOUR FEEDBACK IS IMPORTANT TO US. WE WOULD
APPRECIATEIT IF YOU COULD tAKE A MINUTE TO POST
AN HONEST REVIEW ON AMAZON.

Made in the USA
Las Vegas, NV
08 December 2024

13553995R00046